P
th

PALORES PUBLICATIONS' 21st CENTURY WRITERS

Phil Lucas
Poems From the Seashore

July 2006

ISBN ISBN 0-9551878-3-4
978-0-9551878-34

Published by:

Palores Publications,
11a Penryn Street,
Redruth,
Cornwall.
TR15 2SP

Designed and printed by:

ImageSet,
63 Tehidy Road,
Camborne,
Cornwall.
TR14 8LJ
01209 712864

Typeset in GillSans Light 11/12pt

To my parents

for a lifetime of love,
care and understanding.

Contents

Padstow Night

Sea mist
wraps the creamy whipped
watching gull
who sits and barks
her ocean dreams.
  Taking twilight
under crescent wings
she calls
to a distant
shoreline moonbeam.
  Then silence,
but for
the hushed lullaby
of the tide
  softly rocking
fishing boats
to dreams.

I Can Fall in Love

I can fall in love
with a snowflake
fighting on the wind
and merging in death
with the tar black
crow black
dew pond.

I can fall in love
with a soul searching
street corner teen,
the world at her head
and friends at her feet.

I can fall in love
with the burning shell
of a dying smoke,
unlocking her final puff
and fading
to a snake of ash.

I can fall in love
with an addled rollerblade crack bitch,
her zigzag crazy wit
jaywalking
to oblivion.

I can fall in love
with the purr of the sea
kissing each sand jewelled toe
of a weed drenched beach girl,
the sun combing her hair.

I can fall in love
with the wine blessed fairy
drinking her muddled dreams
into a frost tipped buttercup.

I can fall in love.

Sand

I think it is best
she said
that we write our names
in sand.
Tattoos
are more permanent
   and shun change.

The Bench

It was just Rudy and myself
playing in the first rock pool
of a season's day.
Our feet danced as beach fairies
with the tide's Cornish mantra
and magic sea fizz
conjured merry games
with our rainbow shirts.

Above,
a simple tide brushed bench
where I dozed sometime,
to hold the glow of friendship.
    A carved sun bleached name
'Rudy'
I lay with,
whispering secrets,
through golden cupped hands.

Summer friends
we could have been.

Free For Good

I don't have to look forward to a Friday
or face the melancholy truce of a Sunday Eve.
No more counting weekend hours
till the dreaded bell of Death Monday tolls.
No more smiling at fools,
nodding at dull tales of wasted freedom
or waking nights
sweating their rules into a teardrop pillow.

I might take a walk
on a lonely tide
or tell the sea that I am free.
I may paddle the journey of a thousand miles
with sun kissed sparkle toes
or jive some time with seagulls.
I might sit alone
and watch
a sweeping ballet of swallows
or pass the day with dark deeded rooks.

For I am free
free for good
with the sun and the sea
beside me
and
wishing every shape
were we.

Harlyn Bay, Summer Evening

The shore relaxes
as the setting summer sun
follows the tramp home
of barmy burnt beach lovers
with life's clutter
in stripy bags.

All is quiet now.
There are seagulls
who poke at mysteries
and a lone pink plastic windmill
pines for her 'cheap day return' friend.

Time
for the etch-a-sketch tide
to wipe names of sandy lovers
and criss-cross flip-flop footsteps.
Then,
the final invasion
as an army of doomed sandcastles
await
crumbly destruction.

All will be clean
for tomorrow.

We may miss those days

We may miss those days
on the dunes in July.

Surfboards rode the whispering wisdom
of Father Ocean
and seagulls poked days away
with strand line dreams.

We told secrets to the buttercups
and made sand cake slices with golden fingers.
Those lazy flick-a-magazine days,
smoking in hush by the driftwood pool.
The sun lovers.

We may miss those days.

I Need No More

I need no more
than the laughing wing
of a buttercup
or to ask one daisy
who she loves.
No more than
to kiss each leaf
of a lonely weed
or bid the sunshine
for an hour.
No more than
to watch with love
a seagull's curve
or play hide and seek
with the icing cake tide.

Clubs

I joined
Workaholics Anonymous
but found myself
staying late
every night

I joined
Gamblers Anonymous
but found myself
placing a bet
on being cured

I joined
Alcoholics Anonymous
but found myself
raising a toast
to a new beginning

I joined
Anonymous Anonymous
but
found myself.

Blackbird

When black gnarling fog
curls damp despair
around my faded rainbow soul,
lights go out across the earth.
The sky of God's best pastels
fades to moon vacant night
and trees lie stripped
  like old wartime battlefields,
scarred with the stench of hopelessness.
Yet
one little blackbird
takes the fight
and frees the world
to blue again.

St Ives Branch Line

Dreamy sea days
on the trundle train

dolphins and midriffs
beaches and boats
teacakes and seagulls

and home again.

Now

Green like the rock pool
we touched hands
and threw our secrets
to the sea.
Stony as our secret beach
you left me
taking a holed pebble
in a battered blue January bag.

Now
when daylight ripples
empty hours
seagulls hunt alone.
No more
floating home on weedy dreams
with our smoking sun friend.

Now
just the sound of whispering petals
astray on lanes
where we confessed love,
and streetlights mark the doorway
to a vacant promise
where once we frolicked with twilight.

Now
lonely midnight comes
and gnaws at your perfume pillow
I have to keep.
Turning teardrops to waking hours
and shining moonbeams
on a space
where once a holed pebble kept watch
by a battered blue summer bag.

Falling High

One day you'll fall
says
the dog chasing the kite,
and I'll be there
to get you.
   But the kite
never falls.
It just gets
higher
and higher.

Dreams Alone

My dreams
are stored in a night jar
  so
there is no pain
amongst the moonbeams.
Just
your star lipped voice
falling away
  forever.

I have made plans for my funeral

I wish no suits,
no ties
for that is what they are.
Come only with the weary clothes
of a lazy day
and a pocketful of sweet bird food
for my grave.

Let wild flowers run free
with commotion
and bring nettle, thistle and daisy
so I may doze
with the dance of the butterfly
and taste the bounty of the bee.

Place a bowl of fresh water blue
for my true friend
the blackbird
and let dreamy yard cats sleep
their roving days
amongst my flowered soul.

And place me close
to my old friend the ocean
and let me near her tide
to wash my heart with seashells
and sing forever more
to my dappled midday sun friend.

Seven Bays for Seven Days

Seven rock pools
I counted today.
One for every month
you have been gone.
Seven seagulls
across seven bays
and
seven starfish
lying lonely
on driftwood sands.

At The Airport

I
asked
the
check
in
girl
to
check
out
me,
but
she
said
I
had
excess
baggage.

A Seagull Family Christmas

Their salty cliffside rock home
is adorned
with a good sized branch,
brought home by father's beak
and decorated
with stolen tourist treats.
A little wooden fisherman
sits on top.

Mother seagull
gets into a flap
when thinking of all the fresh fish gifts
she must wrap and deliver,
but outside
there is knocking on a granite door.
Young carol chirpers
are barking for a herring.

At midnight
it is tradition
for all gulls
to collect en masse
for mass.
They squawk age old rhymes
in honour of a mystical bird
who died to save them all.

There is seagull Santa
who wraps himself
in an old red plastic bag
and leaves sand eels for the young
in webbed foot stockings.

Grey mottled babies
lie awake at night
black eyes in wide awe
for the morning
when
nestled up with parents
they open fishy gifts.

I think at 3pm
they gather on the strand
to hear
the ocean give her Christmas speech.

If At All

If at all
when will I see you again?
  Our one meeting,
four smoky hours of wonder,
a thousand ready questions
and
a leaping high-jump heart
still running.

I can only say
I knew,
from your twilight rainbow top,
your hair I long to see framed
on a love blessed sun beach
  and
your silver sea sparkle chat.
      I knew.

You danced
alone
as if a great victory in war
had been sealed.
How I wished courage
to share the rejoicing.
  The band deserved our honour
you said.
What grace in golden meaning.

Now you are gone.
I am forgotten
perhaps
as you dance again
where wonder grows
in a stranger's eyes.
But a careless hope
flutters
these next few days
that luck will click us together.
One more evening
maybe
where you will be mine again.

If at all
when will I see you again?

I Thought...

I thought I heard
your flip-flop footsteps
coming close to me,
   but of course
a stranger,
   another lonely beach girl
with a rucksack of sorrows
crying to the sweet song
of the rock pipit's call
   and wishing
upon a hollow sea.

I thought I saw
your cloud wrapped body
near
on a field of sea lavender,
   but of course
a stranger,
   one more sunshine lover
who nodded hello
and plucked flowers
to take home
and place in a vase called lonely.

I thought I felt
your fairytale true breath
bathing next to me,
   but of course
a stranger,
   just a childish wind
looking for a friend,
kissing moondance curtains
and calling in ripples
to a heart that has lost
her lover.

For Amber

It was good to see you smile again
and dream
a lost dune sunshine
that once held your eyes
as the story of forever.

To have bathed
in the cool
of your ever blackbird voice
and watched your flowered hair
play games with the breeze
and rest.
A polished heart memory
for all time.

There was
the chatter of truths
we had always known,
and laughter,
the only thing
that mattered
in our one
sun dazed summer.

Choosing music
a childish bliss,
 until we parted
to play the same songs
on different journeys home.
I think later
of us singing
on a secret driftwood beach.

The world is a better place
for you
   and I'll keep the memories
in a teardrop heart,
letting the bad times
catch the wind
   and scatter.

Without Light

In the cities
lie hearts made from frowns
where the breeze of glory summer
passes unloved
and people talk their dreams away
in choc-a-block liquid houses.
"Good health" they cheer
as the stout man drinks his stout
the mild man drinks his mild
and
the bitter man
drinks to oblivion,
   seeing only the twilight
of another tortured day.

Safe With The Rain

The wind of star shine midnight
plays
with my little tin home
once more.
Her lover
the rain
leaves gentle
tip-toe kisses upon the roof.
Drifting,
I wish only
a crackly shipping forecast
and then to dream
a sea beat ocean shack
on a tide curved
honeycomb beach.

Pigeons

Pigeons
on the roadside
pecking for a bargain,
plumping up
for a mate,
busying
   bustling
with waste.

Pigeons
in the mirror.

A Sweet View From the Window

A sweet view from the window
keeps cold reality at bay.

Only
the gentle plucking of a turnstone
and the teatime tales
of tar rolled homebound rooks
sun weary
from days in dazzled corn fields.

A misty stream
kisses a creaking bough riverbank
and twenty-one ducks
talk grassy twilight politics,
saluting the setting sun
with watery down wing tips.

Away
a neon kingfisher
and her silver flash bounty
lie cupped in the hands
of the smoky evening oak.

A sweet view from the window
keeps cold reality at bay.

The Line

I've never seen the happy news
the train brings down the line,
I've never seen the laughing ones
the people given time,
to follow loving casually
with never ambushed hearts,
the joyous void inside
that lingers when apart.
I've seen the pain
and what it means
to live when half alive,
and fight the hours
as you move on
when time dictates love dies.

Search Over

I sat shaking at the station,
smoking cigarettes
like a novice Bogart
waiting for your old film arrival,
but you didn't come.

I found a quiet bar
but searched so many more
so I could see your smile
framed,
and bought an antique cross
of amber
to keep your faith with me
always.

And now we've met and parted
I listen to your favourite songs.
The only piece of you
I can keep forever.

Nothing left to say

Nothing left to say
except the words that come
when love dies.
  That love is
more than warmth against cold fright,
more than chosen secrets on a poppy lane,
more even
than understanding.
  Just a little jewelled box
that opens for a while
and two china figures
who sing
until the show is over.

But You Were Gone

I made a golden sand mitten today
then met your eyes
in the wish-wash rock pool.
There were seashells
that sounded your name
faintly
and driftwood to arrange as hope.

Just once
I sang a lullaby with the tide,
and picked a pebble
to offer as sunshine
with your smile.
Near
a crystal tipped sail boat,
blew kisses to the wind.

But you were gone.

London's lost Love

Not even London,
the city of love's fire
could redeem our failure
the night
it all ended.
I mounted a salvage operation
across the Thames,
you sent it to the bottom.
I showed you the towers,
each light a beacon
guiding our love.
You said they were lighthouses
warning us away.
The planes were fireworks
signalling a new beginning,
but like you
they were just reaching
the end of their journey.
To the north Nelson stood in victory
to its south I slumped in defeat.
We made for home,
the silence of the lost
upon us,
and
London
given with tears
to lovers new.

All is Quiet

All is quiet.
Just a breeze
on the gilded rock shore
and mumbling
wishing well penny pebbles.
Just the ripple
of a cloudy seagull
and twilight endeavours
of a sherbet honeybee.
Just loose kisses
from sweet campion fields
and the feathered
dreams of the sky.

All is quiet.